Classic Hymns & Carols

Classic Hymns & Carols

with a Foreword by
John Betjeman

BATSFORD

First published in the United Kingdom in 2012 by
Batsford
10 Southcombe Street
London W14 0RA

This book is based on *Hymns as Poetry* (Batsford, 1980)

An imprint of Anova Books Company Ltd

ISBN: 9781849940474

A CIP catalogue record for this book is available from
the British Library.

20 19 18 17 16 15 14 13 12
10 9 8 7 6 5 4 3 2 1

Reproduction by Mission Productions Ltd, Hong Kong
Printed by 1010 Printing International Ltd, China

This book can be ordered direct from the publisher at the website:
www.anovabooks.com, or try your local bookshop.

Distributed in the United States and Canada
by Sterling Publishing Co.,
387 Park Avenue South, New York, NY 10016, USA

Contents

CAROLS

Foreword by John Betjeman

Our greatest religious poet is Blake. He alone seems to have expressed the Deity in rhythm and metre without being commonplace. In the seventeenth century there were some great poets who wrote religious lyrics: George Herbert, Richard Baxter, Richard Crashaw, Milton, John Byrom. The subject was not too big for them. Isaac Watts is to me the outstanding seventeenth-century hymn writer:

> *When I survey the wondrous Cross*
> *Where the young Prince of glory died.*

The older seventeenth-century lines are, as in this case, often more striking than Victorian revisions of them. That fierce Calvinist, Augustus Montague Toplady (an old Westminster) wrote a final verse to 'Rock of Ages' which was too much for Victorian imaginings:

> *While I draw this fleeting breath,*
> *When my eyestrings break in death.*

This is where English painting, except for Blake, Samuel Palmer and some of the medieval illuminators, falls short of the standards set by seventeenth-century hymn writers. In the painting of sacred subjects there was an almost total gap of about two and a half centuries from the Reformation until Blake was to treat the theme with conviction again. The Pre-Raphaelites as painters seem to me smaller beer and more literary than such poetic giants as Milton.[*]

There were plenty of people who were good poets only as hymn writers, notably JM Neale. Another good poet is Mrs CF Alexander (whose country of Northern Ireland shines through 'All things bright and beautiful'). With some exceptions, such as Cecil Spring-Rice and Kipling's 'Recessional', there has been a decline in the present century in religious poetry, as in religious painting, but overall there is much indeed worth reading and looking at.

John Betjeman (1980)

[*]Although many of us will agree with Dr Johnson's observation: '*Paradise Lost* is one of the books which the reader admires and lays down, and forgets to take up again. None ever wished it longer than it is. Its perusal is a duty rather than a pleasure.'

The Lord
is my shepherd

The Lord is my shepherd; I'll not want.
He makes me down to lie
In pastures green: he leadeth me
The quiet waters by.

My soul he doth restore again;
And me to walk doth make
Within the paths of righteousness,
Even for his own name's sake.

Yea, though I walk in death's dark vale,
Yet will I fear no ill;
For thou art with me; and thy rod
And staff my comfort still.

My table thou hast furnishèd
In presence of my foes;
My head thou dost with oil anoint,
And my cup overflows.

Goodness and mercy all my life
Shall surely follow me;
And in God's house forevermore
My dwelling place shall be.

Psalm 23 translated by
Miles Coverdale (1488–1568)

Ein' feste Burg

A safe stronghold our God is still,
A trusty shield and weapon;
He'll help us clear from all the ill
That hath us now o'ertaken.
The ancient prince of hell
Hath risen with purpose fell;
Strong mail of craft and power
He weareth in this hour;
On earth is not his fellow.

With force of arms we nothing can,
Full soon were we down-ridden;
But for us fights the proper man,
Whom God himself hath bidden.
Ask ye, Who is this same?
Christ Jesus is his name,
The Lord Sabaoth's Son;
He, and no other one,
Shall conquer in the battle.

And were this world all devils o'er
And watching to devour us,
We lay it not to heart so sore;
Not they can overpower us.
And let the prince of ill
Look grim as e'er he will,
He harms us not a whit;
For why? – his doom is writ;
A word shall quickly slay him.

God's word, for all their craft and force,
One moment will not linger,
But, spite of hell, shall have its course;
'Tis written by his finger.
And though they take our life,
Goods, honour, children, wife,
Yet is their profit small;
These things shall vanish all,
The city of God remaineth.

original poem by
Martin Luther (1483–1546)

Jerusalem the golden

Jerusalem the golden,
With milk and honey blest,
Beneath thy contemplation
Sink heart and voice oppressed.
I know not, O I know not,
What joys await us there,
What radiancy of glory,
What bliss beyond compare.

They stand, those halls of Zion,
All jubilant with song,
And bright with many an angel,
And all the martyr throng;
The Prince is ever in them,
The daylight is serene;
The pastures of the blessèd
Are decked in glorious sheen.

There is the throne of David,
And there, from care released,
The shout of them that triumph,
The song of them that feast;
And they, who with their leader,
Have conquered in the fight,
Forever and forever
Are clad in robes of white.

O sweet and blessèd country,
The home of God's elect!
O sweet and blessèd country,
That eager hearts expect!
Jesus, in mercy bring us
To that dear land of rest,
Who art, with God the Father,
And Spirit, ever blessed.

For thee, O dear, dear country,
Mine eyes their vigils keep;
For very love, beholding,
Thy happy name, they weep:
The mention of thy glory
Is unction to the breast,
And medicine in sickness,
And love, and life, and rest.

O one, O only mansion!
O paradise of joy!
Where tears are ever banished,
And smiles have no alloy;
The cross is all thy splendour,
The crucified thy praise,
His laud and benediction
Thy ransomed people raise.

Jerusalem the glorious!
Glory of the elect!
O dear and future vision
That eager hearts expect!
Even now by faith I see thee,

Even here thy walls discern;
To thee my thoughts are kindled,
And strive, and pant, and yearn.

Jerusalem, the only,
That look'st from heaven below,
In thee is all my glory,
In me is all my woe!
And though my body may not,
My spirit seeks thee fain,
Till flesh and earth return me
To earth and flesh again.

When in his strength I struggle,
For very joy I leap;
When in my sin I totter,
I weep, or try to weep:
And grace, sweet grace celestial,
Shall all its love display,
And David's royal fountain
Purge every stain away.

O sweet and blessèd country,
Shall I ever see thy face?
O sweet and blessèd country,
Shall I ever win thy grace?
Exult, O dust and ashes!
The Lord shall be thy part:
His only, his forever
Thou shalt be, and thou art!

original poem by
Bernard of Cluny (12th century)

I will lift up mine eyes unto the hills

Mine eyes look toward the mountains,
Help cometh from on high;
From God who never slumbers,
Whose care is ever nigh.

My foot shall not be movèd,
My keeper is the Lord;
He never shall forsake me;
I trust me to his word.

God keepeth me from falling,
Fulfilleth all my need;
His love doth e'er uphold me,
In faithful word and deed.

He keepeth me from evil,
My onward way doth trace,
My going and my coming,
He crowneth with his grace.

Psalm 121 translated by
Miles Coverdale (1488–1568)

The Lord will come
and not be slow

The Lord will come and not be slow,
His footsteps cannot err;
Before him righteousness shall go,
His royal harbinger.

Mercy and truth, that long were missed,
Now joyfully are met;
Sweet peace and righteousness have kissed,
And hand in hand are set.

Rise, God, judge thou the earth in might,
This wicked earth redress;
For thou art he who shalt by right
The nations all possess.

The nations all whom thou hast made
Shall come, and all shall frame
To bow them low before thee, Lord,
And glorify thy name!

Truth from the earth, like to a flower,
Shall bud and blossom then;
And justice, from her heavenly bower,
Look down on mortal men.

Thee will I praise, O Lord, my God!
Thee honor and adore
With my whole heart; and blaze abroad
Thy name forevermore!

original poem by
John Milton (1608–1674)

Let us with a gladsome mind

Let us with a gladsome mind
Praise the Lord, for he is kind.

Chorus
For his mercies ay endure,
Ever faithful, ever sure.

Let us blaze his name abroad,
For of gods he is the God.

Chorus

He with all-commanding might
Filled the new-made world with light.

Chorus

He hath, with a piteous eye,
Looked upon our misery.

Chorus

He the golden-tressèd sun
Caused all day his course to run.

Chorus

The hornèd moon to shine by night,
'Mid her spangled sisters bright.

Chorus

All things living he doth feed,
His full hand supplies their need.

Chorus

Let us, with a gladsome mind,
Praise the Lord, for he is kind.

Chorus

original poem by
John Milton (1608–1674)

Ye holy angels bright

Ye holy angels bright,
Who stand before God's throne,
And dwell in glorious light,
Praise ye the Lord each one!
Assist our song, or else the theme
Too high doth seem for mortal tongue.

Ye blessèd souls at rest,
That see your Saviour's face,
Whose glory, e'en the least,
Is far above our grace.
God's praises sound, as in his sight
With sweet delight you do abound.

Ye saints, who toil below,
Adore your heavenly King,
And onward as ye go
Some joyful anthem sing;
Take what he gives and praise him still,
Through good or ill, who ever lives!

All nations of the earth,
Extol the world's great King:
With melody and mirth
His glorious praises sing,
For he still reigns, and will bring low
The proudest foe that him disdains.

Sing forth Jehovah's praise,
Ye saints, that on him call!
Him magnify always
His holy churches all!
In him rejoice, and there proclaim
His holy name with sounding voice.

My soul, bear thou thy part,
Triumph in God above!
And with a well-tuned heart
Sing thou the songs of love!
And all my days let no distress
Nor fears suppress his joyful praise.

Away, distrustful care!
I have thy promise, Lord:
To banish all despair,
I have thine oath and word:
And therefore I shall see thy face
And there thy grace shall magnify.

With thy triumphant flock
Then I shall numbered be;
Built on th'eternal rock,
His glory shall we see.
The heav'ns so high
With praise shall ring
And all shall sing in harmony.

original poem by
Richard Baxter (1615–1691)

Lord, it belongs not to my care

Lord, it belongs not to my care
Whether I die or live;
To love and serve thee is my share,
And this thy grace must give.

If life be long, I will be glad,
That I may long obey;
If short, yet why should I be sad
To welcome endless day?

Christ leads me through no darker rooms
Than he went through before;
He that into God's kingdom comes
Must enter by this door.

Come, Lord, when grace hath made me meet
Thy blessèd face to see:
For if thy work on earth be sweet
What will thy glory be!

Then I shall end my sad complaints
And weary, sinful days,
And join with the triumphant saints
That sing my Saviour's praise.

My knowledge of that life is small,
The eye of faith is dim;
But 'tis enough that Christ knows all,
And I shall be with him.

original poem by
Richard Baxter (1615–1691)

Long did I toil

Long did I toil, and knew no earthly rest,
Far did I rove, and found no certain home;
At last I sought them in his sheltering breast,
Who opes his arms, and bids the weary come:
With him I found a home, a rest divine,
And since then I am his, and he is mine.

The good I have is from his stores supplied,
The ill is only what he deems the best;
He for my friend, I'm rich with nought beside,
And poor without him, though of all possessed:
Changes may come, I take, or I resign,
Content, while I am his, while he is mine.

Whate'er may change, in him no change is seen,
A glorious sun that wanes not nor declines;
Above the clouds and storms he walks serene,
And on his people's inward darkness shines:
All may depart, I fret not, nor repine,
While I my Saviour's am, while he is mine.

While here, alas! I know but half his love,
But half discern him, and but half adore;
But when I meet him in the realms above
I hope to love him better, praise him more,
And feel, and tell, amid the choir divine,
How fully I am his, and he is mine.

original poem by
John Quarles (1624–1665) and HF Lyte (1793–1847)

He who would valiant be

He who would valiant be,
'Gainst all disaster;
Let him in constancy,
Follow the master.
There's no discouragement
Shall make him once relent,
His first avowed intent
To be a pilgrim.

Who so beset him round
With dismal stories,
Do but themselves confound,
His strength the more is;
No foes shall stay his might,
Though he with giants fight;
He will make good his right
To be a pilgrim.

Since, Lord, thou dost defend
Us with thy Spirit,
We know he at the end,
Shall life inherit.
Then fancies fly away!
He'll fear not what men say,
He'll labour night and day
To be a pilgrim.

original poem by
John Bunyan (1628–1688)

Let all the world in ev'ry corner sing

Chorus:
Let all the world in ev'ry corner sing,
            My God and King.

    The heav'ns are not too high,
    His praise may thither fly:
    The earth is not too low,
    His praises there may grow.

Chorus

    The church with psalms must shout,
    No door can keep them out:
    But above all, the heart
    Must bear the longest part.

Chorus

original poem by
George Herbert (1593–1632)

Creator Spirit, by whose aid

Creator Spirit, by whose aid
The world's foundations first were laid,
Come, visit every pious mind;
Come, pour thy joys on human kind;
From sin, and sorrow set us free;
And make thy temples worthy thee.

O source of uncreated light,
The Father's promised Paraclete,
Thrice holy fount, thrice holy fire,
Our hearts with heav'nly love inspire;
Come, and thy sacred unction bring
To sanctify us, while we sing.

Plenteous of grace, descend from high
Thou strength of his almighty hand,
Whose pow'r does heav'n and earth command:
Proceeding Spirit, our defense,
Who dost the gift of tongues dispense,
And crown'st thy gift with eloquence!

Refine and purge our earthly parts;
But, oh, inflame and fire our hearts!
Our frailties help, our vice control;
Submit the senses to the soul;
And when rebellious they are grown,
Then, lay thy hand, and hold them down.

Create all new; our wills control,
Subdue the rebel in our soul;
Make us eternal truths receive,
And practice all that we believe;
Give us thyself, that we may see
The Father and the Son by thee.

Immortal honour, endless fame,
Attend th'almighty Father's name;
The Saviour Son be glorified,
Who for lost man's redemption died;
And equal adoration be,
Eternal Paraclete, to thee.

original poem by
John Dryden (1631–1701)

Awake, my soul, and with the sun

Awake, my soul, and with the sun
Thy daily stage of duty run;
Shake off dull sloth, and joyful rise
To pay thy morning sacrifice.

Thy precious time misspent, redeem,
Each present day thy last esteem,
Improve thy talent with due care;
For the great day thyself prepare.

By influence of the light divine
Let thy own light to others shine.
Reflect all heaven's propitious ways
In ardent love and cheerful praise.

In conversation be sincere;
Keep conscience as the noontide clear;
Think how all seeing God thy ways
And all thy secret thoughts surveys.

Wake, and lift up thyself, my heart,
And with the angels bear thy part,
Who all night long unwearied sing
High praise to the eternal King.

Glory to thee, who safe has kept
And hast refreshed me while I slept;
Grant, Lord, when I from death shall wake
I may of endless light partake.

Heav'n is, dear Lord, where'er thou art,
O never then from me depart;
For to my soul 'tis hell to be
But for one moment void of thee.

Lord, I my vows to thee renew;
Scatter my sins as morning dew;
Guard my first springs of thought and will,
And with thyself my spirit fill.

Direct, control, suggest, this day
All I design, or do, or say;
That all my powers, with all their might,
In thy sole glory may unite.

I would not wake nor rise again
And heaven itself I would disdain,
Wert thou not there to be enjoyed,
And I in hymns to be employed.

Praise God, from whom all blessings flow;
Praise him, all creatures here below,
Praise him above, ye heavenly host,
Praise Father, Son, and Holy Ghost.

original poem by
Bishop Thomas Ken (1637–1711)

God, that madest earth and heaven

God, that madest earth and heaven, darkness and light;
Who the day for toil hast given, for rest the night;
May thine angel-guards defend us,
Slumber sweet thy mercy send us,
Holy dreams and hopes attend us,
all through the night.

And when morn again shall call us, to run life's way,
May we still, whatever befall us, thy will obey.
From the power of evil hide us,
In the narrow pathway guide us,
Nor thy smile be ever denied us
all through the day.

Guard us waking, guard us sleeping; And, when we die,
May we in thy mighty keeping all peaceful lie:
When the last dread call shall wake us,
Do not thou our God forsake us,
But to reign in glory take us
with thee on high.

original poem by
Bishop Robert Heber (1783–1826)
and Archbishop Richard Whately (1787–1863)

Glory to thee, my God, this night

Glory to thee, my God, this night
For all the blessings of the light;
Keep me, O keep me, King of kings,
Beneath thine own almighty wings.

Forgive me, Lord, for thy dear Son,
The ill that I this day have done,
That with the world, myself, and thee,
I, ere I sleep, at peace may be.

Teach me to live, that I may dread
The grave as little as my bed.
Teach me to die, that so I may
Rise glorious at the judgment day.

O may my soul on thee repose,
And with sweet sleep mine eyelids close,
Sleep that may me more vigorous make
To serve my God when I awake.

When in the night I sleepless lie,
My soul with heavenly thoughts supply;
Let no ill dreams disturb my rest,
No powers of darkness me molest.

O when shall I, in endless day,
For ever chase dark sleep away,
And hymns divine with angels sing,
All praise to thee, eternal King?

Praise God, from whom all blessings flow,
Praise him, all creatures here below,
Praise him above, ye heavenly host,
Praise Father, Son, and Holy Ghost.

original poem by
Bishop Thomas Ken (1637–1711)

Through all the changing scenes of life

Through all the changing scenes of life,
In trouble and in joy,
The praises of my God shall still
My heart and tongue employ.

Of his deliverance I will boast,
Till all that are distressed
From my example courage take
And soothe their griefs to rest.

O magnify the Lord with me,
With me exalt his name;
When in distress to him I called,
He to my rescue came.

Their drooping hearts were soon refreshed,
Who looked to him for aid;
Desired success in every face,
A cheerful air displayed.

'Behold', they say, 'Behold the man
Whom providence relieved;
The man so dangerously beset,
So wondrously retrieved!'

The hosts of God encamped around
The dwellings of the just;
Deliverance he affords to all
Who on his succour trust.

O make but trial of his love;
Experience will decide
How blest are they, and only they,
Who in his truth confide.

Fear him, ye saints, and you will then
Have nothing else to fear;
Make you his service your delight,
Your wants shall be his care.

While hungry lions lack their prey,
The Lord will food provide
For such as put their trust in him,
And see their needs supplied.

original poem by
Nahum Tate (1652–1715)
and Nicholas Brady (1659–1726)

As pants the hart

As pants the hart for cooling streams
When heated in the chase,
So longs my soul, O God, for thee,
And thy refreshing grace.

For thee, my God, the living God,
My thirsty soul doth pine:
O when shall I behold thy face,
Thou majesty divine!

Why restless, why cast down, my soul?
Hope still, and thou shalt sing
The praise of him who is thy God,
Thy health's eternal spring.

To Father, Son, and Holy Ghost,
The God whom we adore,
Be glory, as it was, is now,
And shall be evermore.

original poem by
Nahum Tate (1652–1715)
and Nicholas Brady (1659–1726)

The spacious firmament on high

The spacious firmament on high,
With all the blue ethereal sky,
And spangled heavens, a shining frame,
Their great original proclaim.
Th'unwearied sun from day to day
Does his creator's powers display,
And publishes to every land
The work of an almighty hand.

Soon as the evening shades prevail,
The moon takes up the wondrous tale;
And nightly to the listening earth,
Repeats the story of her birth;
While all the stars that round her burn,
And all the planets in their turn,
Confirm the tidings, as they roll,
And spread the truth from pole to pole.

What though in solemn silence all
Move round the dark terrestrial ball;
What though no real voice nor sound
Amid the radiant orbs be found?
In reason's ear they all rejoice,
And utter forth a glorious voice;
Forever singing as they shine,
'The hand that made us is divine'.

original poem by
Joseph Addison (1672–1719)

There is a land
of pure delight

There is a land of pure delight
Where saints immortal reign;
Infinite day excludes the night,
And pleasures banish pain.

There everlasting spring abides,
And never-withering flowers:
Death like a narrow sea divides
This heav'nly land from ours.

Sweet fields beyond the swelling flood
Stand dressed in living green:
So to the Jews old Canaan stood,
While Jordan rolled between.

But timorous mortals start and shrink
To cross this narrow sea,
And linger shivering on the brink
And fear to launch away.

O could we make our doubts remove,
Those gloomy thoughts that rise,
And see the Canaan that we love,
With unbeclouded eyes.

Could we but climb where Moses stood,
And view the landscape o'er,
Not Jordan's stream, nor death's cold flood,
Should fright us from the shore.

original poem by
Isaac Watts (1674–1748)

When all
thy mercies, O my God

When all thy mercies, O my God,
My rising soul surveys,
Transported with the view, I'm lost
In wonder, love, and praise.

Thy providence my life sustained,
And all my wants redressed,
While in the silent womb I lay,
And hung upon the breast.

To all my weak complaints and cries
Thy mercy lent an ear,
Ere yet my feeble thoughts had learned
To form themselves in prayer.

Unnumbered comforts to my soul
Thy tender care bestowed,
Before my infant heart conceived
From whom those comforts flowed.

When in the slippery paths of youth
With heedless steps I ran,
Thine arm unseen conveyed me safe,
And led me up to man.

Through hidden dangers, toils, and deaths,
It gently cleared my way;
And through the pleasing snares of vice,
More to be feared than they.

O how shall words with equal warmth
The gratitude declare,
That glows within my ravished heart?
But thou canst read it there.

Thy bounteous hand with worldly bliss
Hath made my cup run o'er;
And, in a kind and faithful friend,
Hath doubled all my store.

Ten thousand thousand precious gifts
My daily thanks employ;
Nor is the last a cheerful heart
That tastes those gifts with joy.

When worn with sickness, oft hast thou
With health renewed my face;
And when in sins and sorrows sunk,
Revived my soul with grace.

Through every period of my life
Thy goodness I'll pursue,
And after death in distant worlds,
The glorious theme renew.

When nature fails, and day and night
Divide thy works no more,
My ever grateful heart, O Lord,
Thy mercy shall adore.

Through all eternity to thee
A joyful song I'll raise;
For Oh! eternity's too short
To utter all thy praise.

original poem by
Joseph Addison (1672–1719)

O God, our help in ages past

O God, our help in ages past,
Our hope for years to come,
Our shelter from the stormy blast,
And our eternal home.

Under the shadow of thy throne
Thy saints have dwelt secure;
Sufficient is thine arm alone,
And our defence is sure.

Before the hills in order stood,
Or earth received her frame,
From everlasting thou art God,
To endless years the same.

Thy word commands our flesh to dust,
'Return, ye sons of men':
All nations rose from earth at first,
And turn to earth again.

A thousand ages in thy sight
Are like an evening gone;
Short as the watch that ends the night
Before the rising sun.

The busy tribes of flesh and blood
With all their lives and cares
Are carried downwards by thy flood
And lost in following years.

Time, like an ever-rolling stream
Bears all its sons away;
They fly forgotten as a dream
Dies at the opening day.

Like flowery fields the nations stand
Pleased with the morning light;
The flowers beneath the mower's hand
Lie withering ere 'tis night.

O God, our help in ages past,
Our hope for years to come,
Be thou our guard while life shall last,
And our eternal home.

original poem by
Isaac Watts (1674–1748)

Jesus shall reign where'er the sun

Jesus shall reign where'er the sun
Does his successive journeys run;
His kingdom stretch from shore to shore,
Till moons shall wax and wane no more.

Behold the islands with their kings,
And Europe her best tribute brings;
From north to south the princes meet,
To pay their homage at his feet.

There Persia, glorious to behold,
There India shines in eastern gold;
And barb'rous nations at his word
Submit, and bow, and own their Lord.

To him shall endless prayer be made,
And praises throng to crown his head;
His name like sweet perfume shall rise
With every morning sacrifice.

People and realms of every tongue
Dwell on his love with sweetest song,
And infant voices shall proclaim
Their early blessings on his name.

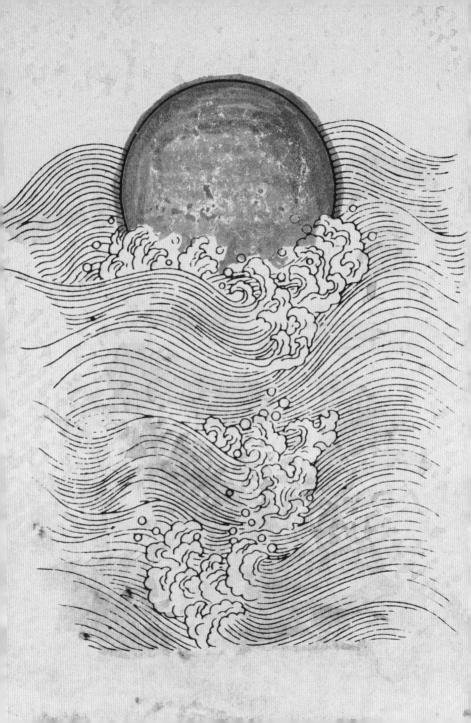

Blessings abound wherever he reigns;
The prisoner leaps to lose his chains;
The weary find eternal rest,
And all the sons of want are blessed.

Where he displays his healing power,
Death and the curse are known no more:
In him the tribes of Adam boast
More blessings than their father lost.

Let every creature rise and bring
Peculiar honours to our King;
Angels descend with songs again,
And earth repeat the loud amen.

Great God, whose universal sway
The known and unknown worlds obey,
Now give the kingdom to thy Son,
Extend his power, exalt his throne.

The sceptre well becomes his hands;
All heav'n submits to his commands;
His justice shall avenge the poor,
And pride and rage prevail no more.

With power he vindicates the just,
And treads th'oppressor in the dust:
His worship and his fear shall last
Till hours, and years, and time be past.

As rain on meadows newly mown,
So shall he send his influence down:
His grace on fainting souls distills,
Like heav'nly dew on thirsty hills.

The heathen lands, that lie beneath
The shades of overspreading death,
Revive at his first dawning light;
And deserts blossom at the sight.

The saints shall flourish in his days,
Dressed in the robes of joy and praise;
Peace, like a river, from his throne
Shall flow to nations yet unknown.

original poem by
Isaac Watts (1674–1748)

O for a thousand tongues to sing

O for a thousand tongues to sing
My great redeemer's praise,
The glories of my God and King,
The triumphs of his grace!

My gracious master and my God,
Assist me to proclaim
And spread through all the earth abroad
The honours of thy name.

Jesus – the name that charms our fears,
That bids our sorrows cease;
'Tis music in the sinner's ears,
'Tis life, and health, and peace.

He breaks the power of cancelled sin,
He sets the prisoner free;
His blood can make the foulest clean;
His blood availed for me.

He speaks; and, listening to his voice,
New life the dead receive,
The mournful broken hearts rejoice,
The humble poor believe.

Hear him, ye deaf; his praise, ye dumb,
Your loosened tongues employ;
Ye blind, behold your Saviour come,
And leap, ye lame, for joy!

In Christ your head, you then shall know,
Shall feel your sins forgiven;
Anticipate your heaven below,
And own that love is heaven.

Glory to God, and praise and love
Be ever, ever given,
By saints below and saints above,
The church in earth and heaven.

On this glad day the glorious sun
Of righteousness arose;
On my benighted soul he shone
And filled it with repose.

Sudden expired the legal strife,
'Twas then I ceased to grieve;
My second, real, living life
I then began to live.

Then with my heart I first believed,
Believed with faith divine,
Power with the Holy Ghost received
To call the Saviour mine.

I felt my Lord's atoning blood
Close to my soul applied;
Me, me he loved, the Son of God,
For me, for me he died!

I found and owned his promise true,
Ascertained of my part,
My pardon passed in heaven I knew
When written on my heart.

Look unto him, ye nations, own
Your God, ye fallen race;
Look, and be saved through faith alone,
Be justified by grace.

See all your sins on Jesus laid:
The Lamb of God was slain,
His soul was once an offering made
For every soul of man.

Harlots and publicans and thieves
In holy triumph join!
Saved is the sinner that believes
From crimes as great as mine.

Murderers and all ye hellish crew
In holy triumph join!
Believe the Saviour died for you;
For me the Saviour died.

With me, your chief, ye then shall know,
Shall feel your sins forgiven;
Anticipate your heaven below,
And own that love is heaven.

original poem by
Charles Wesley (1707–1788)

O for a heart to praise my God

O for a heart to praise my God,
A heart from sin set free;
A heart that always feels thy blood
So freely shed for me:

A heart resigned, submissive, meek,
My great redeemer's throne;
Where only Christ is heard to speak,
Where Jesus reigns alone:

A humble, lowly, contrite heart,
Believing, true and clean,
Which neither life nor death can part
From Christ who dwells within:

A heart in every thought renewed,
And full of love divine;
Perfect, and right and pure, and good,
A copy, Lord, of thine.

Thy tender heart is still the same,
And melts at human woe:
Jesus, for thee distressed I am,
I want thy love to know.

My heart, thou know'st, can never rest
Till thou create my peace;
Till of mine Eden repossest,
From self, and sin, I cease.

Fruit of thy gracious lips, on me
Bestow that peace unknown,
The hidden manna, and the tree
Of life, and the white stone.

Thy nature, gracious Lord, impart,
Come quickly from above;
Write thy new name upon my heart,
Thy new best name of love.

original poem by
Charles Wesley (1707–1788)

Hark, my soul! It is the Lord

Hark, my soul! It is the Lord;
'Tis thy Saviour, hear his word;
Jesus speaks, and speaks to thee:
'Say, poor sinner, lovest thou me?

'I delivered thee when bound,
And, when bleeding, healed thy wound;
Sought thee wandering, set thee right,
Turned thy darkness into light.

'Can a woman's tender care
Cease toward the child she bare?
Yes, she may forgetful be,
Yet will I remember thee.

'Mine is an unchanging love,
Higher than the heights above,
Deeper than the depths beneath,
Free and faithful, strong as death.

'Thou shalt see my glory soon,
When the work of grace is done;
Partner of my throne shalt be:
Say, poor sinner, lovest thou me?'

Lord, it is my chief complaint
That my love is weak and faint;
Yet I love thee, and adore;
O for grace to love thee more!

original poem by
William Cowper (1731–1800)

Retirement

Far from the world, O Lord, I flee,
From strife and tumult far;
From scenes, where Satan wages still
His most successful war.

The calm retreat, the silent shade,
With prayer and praise agree;
And seem by thy sweet bounty made,
For those who follow thee.

There if thy Spirit touch the soul,
And grace her mean abode;
Oh with what peace, and joy, and love
She communes with her God!

There like the nightingale she pours
Her solitary lays;
Nor asks a witness of her song,
Nor thirsts for human praise.

Author and guardian of my life,
Sweet source of light divine;
And (all harmonious names in one)
My Saviour, thou art mine!

What thanks I owe thee, and what love,
A boundless, endless store,
Shall echo through the realms above,
When time shall be no more.

original poem by
William Cowper (1731–1800)

Glorious things of thee are spoken

Glorious things of thee are spoken,
Zion, city of our God!
He whose word cannot be broken
Formed thee for his own abode:
On the Rock of Ages founded,
What can shake thy sure repose?
With salvation's walls surrounded,
Thou may'st smile at all thy foes.

See! the streams of living waters,
Springing from eternal love,
Well supply thy sons and daughters,
And all fear of want remove:
Who can faint while such a river
Ever flows their thirst to assuage?
Grace, which like the Lord the giver,
Never fails from age to age.

Round each habitation hovering,
See the cloud and fire appear!
For a glory and a cov'ring
Showing that the Lord is near.

Thus deriving from our banner
Light by night and shade by day;
Safe they feed upon the manna
Which he gives them when they pray.

Blest inhabitants of Zion,
Washed in the redeemer's blood!
Jesus, whom their souls rely on,
Makes them kings and priests to God.
'Tis his love his people raises,
Over self to reign as kings,
And as priests, his solemn praises
Each for a thank offering brings.

Saviour, if of Zion's city
I, through grace, a member am,
Let the world deride or pity,
I will glory in thy name:
Fading is the worldling's pleasure,
All his boasted pomp and show;
Solid joys and lasting treasure
None but Zion's children know.

original poem by
John Newton (1725–1807)

God moves in a mysterious way

God moves in a mysterious way
His wonders to perform;
He plants his footsteps in the sea
And rides upon the storm.

Deep in unfathomable mines
Of never-failing skill
He treasures up his bright designs,
And works his sovereign will.

Ye fearful saints, fresh courage take,
The clouds ye so much dread
Are big with mercy, and shall break
In blessings on your head.

Judge not the Lord by feeble sense,
But trust him for his grace;
Behind a frowning providence
He hides a smiling face.

His purposes will ripen fast,
Unfolding every hour;
The bud may have a bitter taste,
But sweet will be the flower.

Blind unbelief is sure to err,
And scan his work in vain;
God is his own interpreter,
And he will make it plain.

original poem by
William Cowper (1731–1800)

O for a closer walk with God

O for a closer walk with God,
A calm and heavenly frame;
A light to shine upon the road
That leads me to the Lamb!

Where is the blessedness I knew,
When first I saw the Lord?
Where is the soul refreshing view
Of Jesus and his word?

What peaceful hours I once enjoyed!
How sweet their memory still!
But they have left an aching void
The world can never fill.

Return, O holy dove, return,
Sweet messenger of rest;
I hate the sins that made thee mourn,
And drove thee from my breast.

The dearest idol I have known,
Whate'er that idol be,
Help me to tear it from thy throne,
And worship only thee.

So shall my walk be close with God,
Calm and serene my frame;
So purer light shall mark the road
That leads me to the Lamb.

original poem by
William Cowper (1731–1800)

O thou from whom all goodness flows

O thou from whom all goodness flows,
I lift my heart to thee;
In all my sorrows, conflicts, woes,
Dear Lord, remember me.

When groaning on my burdened heart
My sins lie heavily,
My pardon speak, new peace impart;
In love remember me.

Temptations sore obstruct my way,
And ills I cannot flee:
O give me strength, Lord, as my day;
For good remember me.

Distressed with pain, disease, and grief,
This feeble body see;
Grant patience, rest, and kind relief:
Hear and remember me.

If on my face, for thy dear name,
Shame and reproaches be,
All hail reproach, and welcome shame,
If thou remember me.

The hour is near; consigned to death,
I own the just decree;
'Saviour', with my last parting breath
I'll cry, 'Remember me'.

original poem by
Thomas Haweis (1732–1820)

Jesus, lover of my soul

Jesus, lover of my soul,
Let me to thy bosom fly,
While the nearer waters roll,
While the tempest still is high.

Hide me, O my Saviour, hide,
'Til the storm of life is past;
Safe into the haven guide,
O receive my soul at last.

Other refuge have I none,
Hangs my helpless soul on thee;
Leave, ah! leave me not alone,
Still support and comfort me.

All my trust on thee is stayed,
All my help from thee I bring;
Cover my defenseless head
With the shadow of thy wing.

Wilt thou not regard my call?
Wilt thou not accept my prayer?
Lo! I sink, I faint, I fall – lo!
On thee I cast my care;

Reach me out thy gracious hand!
While I of thy strength receive,
Hoping against hope I stand, dying,
And behold, I live.

Thou, O Christ, art all I want;
More than all in thee I find:
Raise the fallen, cheer the faint,
Heal the sick, and lead the blind.

Just and holy is thy name;
I am all unrighteousness;
False and full of sin I am,
Thou art full of truth and grace.

Plenteous grace with thee is found,
Grace to cover all my sin;
Let the healing streams abound;
Make and keep me pure within.

Thou of life the fountain art;
Freely let me take of thee;
Spring thou up within my heart,
Rise to all eternity.

original poem by
Charles Wesley (1707–1788)

Rock of Ages

Rock of Ages, cleft for me,
Let me hide myself in thee!
Let the water and the blood
From thy wounded side which flowed,
Be of sin the double cure,
Save from wrath and make me pure.

Not the labour of my hands
Can fulfill thy law's demands;
Could my zeal no respite know,
Could my tears forever flow,
All for sin could not atone;
Thou must save, and thou alone.

Nothing in my hand I bring;
Simply to thy cross I cling;
Naked, come to thee for dress;
Helpless, look to thee for grace;
Foul, I to the fountain fly;
Wash me, Saviour, or I die!

While I draw this fleeting breath,
When mine eyes shall close in death,
When I soar to worlds unknown,
See thee on thy judgment-throne,
Rock of Ages, cleft for me,
Let me hide myself in thee!

original poem by
Augustus Montague Toplady (1740–1778)

A cradle song

Sweet dreams, form a shade
O'er my lovely infant's head:
Sweet dreams of pleasant streams
By happy, silent, moony beams.

Sweet sleep, with soft down
Weave thy brows an infant crown.
Sweet sleep, angel mild,
Hover o'er my happy child.

Sweet smiles, in the night
Hover over my delight!
Sweet smiles, mother's smile,
All the livelong night beguile.

Sweet moans, dovelike sighs,
Chase not slumber from thine eyes!
Sweet moan, sweeter smile,
All the dovelike moans beguile.

Sleep, sleep, happy child,
All creation slept and smiled;
Sleep, sleep, happy sleep,
While o'er thee thy mother weep.

Sweet babe, in thy face
Holy image I can trace.
Sweet babe, once like thee,
Thy maker lay, and wept for me.

Wept for me, for thee, for all,
When he was an infant small.
Thou his image ever see,
Heavenly face that smiles on thee.

Smiles on thee, on me, on all;
Who became an infant small.
Infant smiles are his own smiles;
Heaven and earth to peace beguiles.

original poem by
William Blake (1757–1827)

O worship the King

O worship the King all glorious above;
O gratefully sing his power and his love;
Our shield and defender, the ancient of days,
Pavilioned in splendour, and girded with praise.

O tell of his might, O sing of his grace,
Whose robe is the light, whose canopy space.
His chariots of wrath the deep thunderclouds form,
And dark is his path on the wings of the storm.

The earth with its store of wonders untold,
Almighty, thy power hath founded of old;
Established it fast by a changeless decree,
And round it hath cast, like a mantle, the sea.

Thy bountiful care what tongue can recite?
It breathes in the air, it shines in the light;
It streams from the hills, it descends to the plain,
And sweetly distills in the dew and the rain.

Frail children of dust, and feeble as frail,
In thee do we trust, nor find thee to fail:
Thy mercies how tender! How firm to the end!
Our maker, defender, redeemer, and friend.

O measureless might, ineffable love,
While angels delight to worship thee above,
Thy humbler creation, though feeble their lays,
With true adoration shall all sing thy praise.

original poem by
Sir Robert Grant (1779–1838)

To mercy, pity, peace, and love

To mercy, pity, peace, and love,
All pray in their distress,
And to these virtues of delight
Return their thankfulness.

For mercy, pity, peace, and love,
Is God our Father dear;
And mercy, pity, peace, and love,
Is man, his child and care.

For mercy has a human heart,
Pity, a human face;
And love, the human form divine,
And peace, the human dress.

Then every man, of every clime,
That prays in his distress,
Prays to the human form divine:
Love, mercy, pity, peace.

And all must love the human form,
In heathen, Turk or Jew;
Where mercy, love, and pity dwell,
There God is dwelling too.

original poem by
William Blake (1757–1827)

Jerusalem

And did those feet in ancient time
Walk upon England's mountains green?
And was the holy Lamb of God
On England's pleasant pastures seen?
And did the countenance divine
Shine forth upon our clouded hills?
And was Jerusalem builded here,
Among these dark satanic mills?

Bring me my bow of burning gold!
Bring me my arrows of desire!
Bring me my spear! O clouds, unfold!
Bring me my chariot of fire!
I will not cease from mental fight,
Nor shall my sword sleep in my hand,
Till we have built Jerusalem
In England's green and pleasant land.

original poem by
William Blake (1757–1827)

The labourer's noon-day hymn

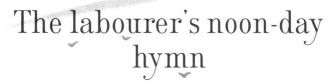

Up to the throne of God is borne
The voice of praise at early morn,
And he accepts the punctual hymn
Sung as the light of day grows dim:

Nor will he turn his ear aside
From holy offerings at noontide:
Then here reposing let us raise
A song of gratitude and praise.

What though our burthen be not light,
We need not toil from morn to night;
The respite of the mid-day hour
Is in the thankful creature's power.

Blest are the moments, doubly blest,
That, drawn from this one hour of rest,
Are with a ready heart bestowed
Upon the service of our God!

Each field is then a hallowed spot,
An altar is in each man's cot,
A church in every grove that spreads
Its living roof above our heads.

Look up to heaven! the industrious sun
Already half his race hath run;
'He cannot halt nor go astray,
But our immortal spirits may.

Lord, since his rising in the east,
If we have faltered or transgressed,
Guide, from thy love's abundant source,
What yet remains of this day's course;

Help with thy grace, through life's short day,
Our upward and our downward way;
And glorify for us the west,
When we shall sink to final rest.

original poem by
William Wordsworth (1770–1850)

When wilt thou save the people

When wilt thou save the people
O God of mercy, when?
Not kings and lords, but nations,
Not thrones and crowns, but men!
Flowers of thy heart, O God, are they;
Let them not pass, like weeds, away.
Their heritage a sunless day.
God, save the people!

Shall crime bring crime forever,
Strength aiding still the strong?
Is it thy will, O Father,
That man shall toil for wrong?
'No,' say thy mountains; 'No,' thy skies;
Man's clouded sun shall brightly rise,
And songs be heard, instead of sighs:
O God, save the people!

When wilt thou save the people?
O God of mercy, when?
The people, Lord, the people,
Not thrones and crowns, but men!
God save the people; thine they are,
Thy children, as thy angels fair:
From vice, oppression, and despair,
O God, save the people!

original poem by
Ebenezer Elliott (1781–1840)

The head that was once crowned with thorns

The head that once was crowned with thorns
Is crowned with glory now:
A royal diadem adorns
The mighty victor's brow.

The highest place that heav'n affords
Belongs to him by right;
The King of kings and Lord of lords,
And heaven's eternal light;

The joy of all who dwell above,
The joy of all below,
To whom he manifests his love,
And grants his name to know.

To them the cross, with all its shame,
With all its grace is given:
Their name an everlasting name,
Their joy the joy of heaven.

They suffer with their Lord below,
They reign with him above,
Their profit and their joy to know
The mystery of his love.

The cross he bore is life and health,
Though shame and death to him;
His people's hope, his people's wealth,
Their everlasting theme.

original poem by
Thomas Kelly (1769–1854)

Christian, dost thou see them

Christian, dost thou see them on the holy ground,
How the powers of darkness rage thy steps around?
Christian, up and smite them, counting gain but loss;
In the strength that cometh by the holy cross.

Christian, dost thou feel them, how they work within,
Striving, tempting, luring, goading into sin?
Christian, never tremble; never be downcast;
Gird thee for the battle, watch and pray and fast.

Christian, dost thou hear them, how they speak thee fair?
'Always fast and vigil? Always watch and prayer?'
Christian, answer boldly, 'While I breathe, I pray':
Peace shall follow battle, night shall end in day.

'Well I know thy trouble, O my servant true;
Thou art very weary – I was weary, too;
But that toil shall make thee some day all mine own –
At the end of sorrow shall be near my throne.'

original poem by
JM Neale (1818–1866)

Worship the Lord

Worship the Lord in the beauty of holiness!
Bow down before him, his glory proclaim;
Gold of obedience, and incense of lowliness,
Bring and adore him, the Lord is his name.

Low at his feet lay thy burden of carefulness,
High on his heart he will bear it for thee,
Comfort thy sorrows, and answer thy prayerfulness,
Guiding thy steps as may best for thee be.

Fear not to enter his courts in the slenderness
Of the poor wealth thou wouldst reckon as thine:
Truth in its beauty, and love in its tenderness,
These are the offerings to lay on his shrine.

These, though we bring them in trembling and fearfulness,
He will accept for the name that is dear;
Mornings of joy give for evenings of tearfulness,
Trust for our trembling and hope for our fear.

original poem by
JSB Monsell (1811–1875)

Our blest redeemer,
ere he breathed

Our blest redeemer, ere he breathed
His tender last farewell,
A guide, a comforter, bequeathed
With us to dwell.

He came in semblance of a dove,
With sheltering wings outspread,
The holy balm of peace and love
On earth to shed.

He came in tongues of living flame,
To teach, convince, subdue;
All-powerful as the wind he came,
As viewless too.

He came sweet influence to impart,
A gracious, willing guest,
While he can find one humble heart
Wherein to rest.

And his that gentle voice we hear,
Soft as the breath of even,
That checks each fault, that calms each fear,
And speaks of heav'n.

And every virtue we possess,
And every conquest won,
And every thought of holiness,
Are his alone.

Spirit of purity and grace,
Our weakness, pitying, see:
O make our hearts thy dwelling-place
And worthier thee.

original poem by
Harriet Auber (1773–1862)

There is a book
who runs may read

There is a book who runs may read,
Which heav'nly truth imparts,
And all the lore its scholars need,
Pure eyes and Christian hearts.

The works of God above, below,
Within us and around,
Are pages in that book, to show
How God himself is found.

The glorious sky, embracing all,
Is like the maker's love,
Wherewith encompassed, great and small
In peace and order move.

The moon above, the church below,
A wondrous race they run;
But all their radiance, all their glow,
Each borrows of its sun.

The Saviour lends the light and heat
That crown his holy hill;
The saints, like stars, around his seat
Perform their courses still.

The saints above are stars in heaven –
What are the saints on earth?
Like trees they stand whom God has given,
Our Eden's happy birth.

Faith is their fixed, unswerving root,
Hope their unfading flower,
Fair deeds of charity their fruit,
The glory of their bower.

The dew of heav'n is like thy grace,
It steals in silence down;
But where it lights, the favoured place,
By richest fruits is known.

One name, above all glorious names,
With its ten thousand tongues
The everlasting sea proclaims,
Echoing angelic songs.

The raging fire, the roaring wind,
Thy boundless power display;
But in the gentler breeze we find
The Spirit's viewless way.

Two worlds are ours: 'tis only sin
Forbids us to descry
The mystic heaven and earth within,
Plain as the sea and sky.

Thou, who hast giv'n me eyes to see
And love this sight so fair,
Give me a heart to find out thee,
And read thee everywhere.

original poem by
John Keble (1792–1866)

Brightest and best of
the sons of the morning

Brightest and best of the sons of the morning,
Dawn on our darkness and lend us thine aid;
Star of the east, the horizon adorning,
Guide where our infant redeemer is laid.

Cold on his cradle the dewdrops are shining,
Low lies his head with the beasts of the stall:
Angels adore him in slumber reclining,
Maker and monarch and Saviour of all.

Say, shall we yield him, in costly devotion,
Odors of Edom and offerings divine?
Gems of the mountain and pearls of the ocean,
Myrrh from the forest or gold from the mine?

Vainly we offer each ample oblation,
Vainly with gifts would his favour secure;
Richer by far is the heart's adoration,
Dearer to God are the prayers of the poor.

original poem by
Bishop Robert Heber (1783–1826)

Lord, I would own thy tender care

Lord, I would own thy tender care,
And all thy love to me;
The food I eat, the clothes I wear,
Are all bestowed by thee.

'Tis thou preservest me from death
And dangers every hour;
I cannot draw another breath
Unless thou give me power.

Kind angels guard me every night,
As round my bed they stay;
Nor am I absent from thy sight
In darkness or by day.

My health and friends and parents dear
To me by God are giv'n;
I have not any blessing here
But what is sent from heav'n.

Such goodness, Lord, and constant care,
I never can repay;
But may it be my daily prayer
To love thee and obey.

original poem by
Jane Taylor (1783–1824)

New every morning is the love

New every morning is the love
Our wakening and uprising prove;
Through sleep and darkness safely brought,
Restored to life, and power, and thought.

New mercies, each returning day,
Hover around us while we pray;
New perils past, new sins forgiven,
New thoughts of God, new hopes of heaven.

If on our daily course our mind
Be set to hallow all we find,
New treasures still, of countless price,
God will provide for sacrifice.

Old friends, old scenes, will lovelier be,
As more of heaven in each we see;
Some softening gleam of love and prayer
Shall dawn on every cross and care.

We need not bid, for cloistered cell,
Our neighbour and our work farewell,
Nor strive to find ourselves too high
For sinful man beneath the sky:

The trivial round, the common task,
Will furnish all we ought to ask –
Room to deny ourselves, a road
To bring us daily nearer God.

Seek we no more; content with these,
Let present rapture, comfort, ease –
As heaven shall bid them, come and go:
The secret this of rest below.

Only, O Lord, in thy dear love
Fit us for perfect rest above;
And help us this and every day
To live more nearly as we pray.

original poem by
John Keble (1792–1866)

Abide with me

Abide with me; fast falls the eventide;
The darkness deepens; Lord, with me abide!
When other helpers fail, and comforts flee,
Help of the helpless, O abide with me.

Swift to its close ebbs out life's little day;
Earth's joys grow dim; its glories pass away;
Change and decay in all around I see;
O thou who changest not, abide with me.

Not a brief glance I beg, a passing word;
But as thou dwell'st with thy disciples, Lord,
Familiar, condescending, patient, free.
Come not to sojourn, but abide with me.

Come not in terrors, as the King of kings,
But kind and good, with healing in thy wings,
Tears for all woes, a heart for every plea –
Come, friend of sinners, and thus bide with me.

Thou on my head in early youth didst smile;
And, though rebellious and perverse meanwhile,
Thou hast not left me, oft as I left thee,
On to the close, O Lord, abide with me.

I need thy presence every passing hour;
What but thy grace can foil the tempter's power?
Who like thyself my guide and stay can be?
Through cloud and sunshine, O abide with me.

I fear no foe with thee at hand to bless;
Ills have no weight, and tears no bitterness.
Where is death's sting? Where, grave, thy victory?
I triumph still, if thou abide with me.

Hold thou thy cross before my closing eyes;
Shine through the gloom, and point me to the skies;
Heaven's morning breaks, and earth's vain shadows flee;
In life, in death, O Lord, abide with me!

original poem by
HF Lyte (1793–1847)

Lead, kindly light

Lead, kindly light, amid th'encircling gloom,
Lead thou me on;
The night is dark, and I am far from home,
Lead thou me on.
Keep thou my feet; I do not ask to see
The distant scene; one step enough for me.

I was not ever thus, nor prayed that thou
Shouldst lead me on;
I loved to choose and see my path; but now
Lead thou me on.
I loved the garish day, and, spite of fears,
Pride ruled my will: remember not past years.

So long thy power hath blest me, sure it still
Will lead me on
O'er moor and fen, o'er crag and torrent, 'til
The night is gone,
And with the morn those angel faces smile,
Which I have loved long since, and lost awhile.

Meantime, along the narrow rugged path,
Thyself hast trod,
Lead, Saviour, lead me home in childlike faith,
Home to my God.
To rest forever after earthly strife
In the calm light of everlasting life.

original poem by
Cardinal JH Newman (1801–1890)

A few more years shall roll

A few more years shall roll,
A few more seasons come,
And we shall be with those that rest
Asleep within the tomb.
Then, O my Lord, prepare
My soul for that great day;

Chorus
O wash me in thy precious blood,
And take my sins away.

A few more suns shall set
O'er these dark hills of time,
And we shall be where suns are not,
A far serener clime.
Then, O my Lord, prepare
My soul for that blest day;

Chorus

A few more storms shall beat
On this wild rocky shore,
And we shall be where tempests cease,
And surges swell no more.
Then, O my Lord, prepare
My soul for that calm day;

Chorus

A few more struggles here,
A few more partings o'er,
A few more toils, a few more tears,
And we shall weep no more.
Then, O my Lord, prepare
My soul for that bright day;

Chorus

A few more Sabbaths here
Shall cheer us on our way,
And we shall reach the endless rest,
Th'eternal Sabbath day.
Then, O my Lord, prepare
My soul for that sweet day;

Chorus

'Tis but a little while
And he shall come again,
Who died that we might live, who lives
That we with him may reign.
Then, O my Lord, prepare
My soul for that glad day;

Chorus

original poem by
Horatius Bonar (1808–1889)

Strong Son of God

Strong Son of God, immortal love,
Whom we, that have not seen thy face,
By faith, and faith alone, embrace,
Believing where we cannot prove:

Thou wilt not leave us in the dust;
Thou madest man, he knows not why;
He thinks he was not made to die:
And thou hast made him, thou art just.

Thou seemest human and divine,
The highest, holiest manhood thou:
Our wills are ours, we know not how;
Ours wills are ours, to make them thine.

Our little systems have their day;
They have their day and cease to be:
They are but broken lights of thee,
And thou, O Lord, art more than they.

We have but faith: we cannot know;
For knowledge is of things we see;
And yet we trust it comes from thee,
A beam in darkness: let it grow.

Let knowledge grow from more to more,
But more of reverence in us dwell;
That mind and soul, according well,
May make one music as before.

But vaster. We are fools and slight;
We mock thee when we do not fear;
But help thy foolish ones to bear –
Help thy vain worlds to bear thy light.

original poem by
Alfred, Lord Tennyson (1809–1892)

Chorus
All things bright and beautiful,
All creatures great and small,
All things wise and wonderful,
The Lord God made them all.

Each little flower that opens,
Each little bird that sings,
He made their glowing colours,
He made their tiny wings.

Chorus

The rich man in his castle,
The poor man at his gate,
He made them, high or lowly,
And ordered their estate.

Chorus

The purple headed mountains,
The river running by,
The sunset and the morning,
That brightens up the sky.

Chorus

The cold wind in the winter,
The pleasant summer sun,
The ripe fruits in the garden,
He made them every one.

Chorus

The tall trees in the greenwood,
The meadows where we play,
The rushes by the water,
To gather every day.

Chorus

He gave us eyes to see them,
And lips that we might tell
How great is God Almighty,
Who has made all things well.

Chorus

original poem by
Cecil F Alexander (1818–1895)

There is a green hill far away

There is a green hill far away,
Outside a city wall,
Where the dear Lord was crucified
Who died to save us all.

Chorus
O dearly, dearly, has he loved,
And we must love him, too,
And trust in his redeeming blood,
And try his works to do.

We may not know, we cannot tell,
What pains he had to bear,
But we believe it was for us
He hung and suffered there.

Chorus

He died that we might be forgiv'n,
He died to make us good;
That we might go at last to heav'n,
Saved by his precious blood.

Chorus

There was no other good enough
To pay the price of sin;
He only could unlock the gate
Of heaven, and let us in.

Chorus

O dearly, dearly has he loved,
And we must love him too,
And trust in his redeeming blood
And try his works to do.

Chorus

original poem by
Cecil F Alexander (1818–1895)

God of our fathers, known of old

God of our fathers, known of old,
Lord of our far-flung battleline,
Beneath whose awful hand we hold
Dominion over palm and pine –
Lord God of hosts, be with us yet,
Lest we forget – lest we forget!

The tumult and the shouting dies;
The captains and the kings depart:
Still stands thine ancient sacrifice,
An humble and a contrite heart.
Lord God of hosts, be with us yet,
Lest we forget – lest we forget!

Far-called, our navies melt away;
On dune and headland sinks the fire:
Lo, all our pomp of yesterday
Is one with Nineveh and Tyre!
Judge of the nations, spare us yet,
Lest we forget – lest we forget!

If, drunk with sight of power, we loose
Wild tongues that have not thee in awe,
Such boastings as the gentiles use
Or lesser breeds without the law –
Lord God of hosts, be with us yet
Lest we forget – lest we forget!

For heathen heart that puts her trust
In reeking tube and iron shard,
All valiant dust that builds on dust,
And guarding, calls not thee to guard,
For frantic boast and foolish word –
Thy mercy on thy people, Lord!

original poem by
Rudyard Kipling (1865–1936)

Art thou weary,
art thou languid

Art thou weary, art thou languid,
Art thou sore distressed?
'Come to me,' saith One, 'and coming
Be at rest'.

Hath he marks to lead me to him,
If he be my guide?
'In his feet and hands are wound prints
And his side.'

Is there diadem as monarch
That his brow adorns?
'Yes, a crown, in very surety,
But of thorns.'

If I find him, if I follow,
What his guerdon here?
'Many a sorrow, many a labour,
Many a tear.'

If I still hold closely to him,
What hath he at last?
'Sorrow vanquished, labour ended,
Jordan passed.'

If I ask him to receive me,
Will he say me nay?
'Not till earth, and not till heaven
Pass away.'

Finding, following, keeping, struggling,
Is he sure to bless?
'Saints, apostles, prophets, martyrs,
Answer, Yes!'

original poem by
JM Neale (1818–1866)

That day of wrath, that dreadful day

That day of wrath, that dreadful day,
When heav'n and earth shall pass away,
What pow'r shall be the sinner's stay?
How shall he meet that dreadful day?

When, shrivelling like a parchèd scroll,
The flaming heav'ns together roll;
When louder yet, and yet more dread,
Swells the high trump that wakes the dead:

O, on that day, that wrathful day,
When man to judgment wakes from clay,
Be thou the trembling sinner's stay,
Though heav'n and earth shall pass away!

original poem by
Sir Walter Scott (1771–1832)

For all the saints

For all the saints who from their labours rest,
Who thee by faith before the world confessed,
Thy name, O Jesus, be forever blessed.
Alleluia, Alleluia!

Thou wast their rock, their fortress, and their might;
Thou, Lord, their captain in the well-fought fight;
Thou in the darkness drear their one true light.
Alleluia, Alleluia!

For the apostles' glorious company,
Who bearing forth the cross o'er land and sea,
Shook all the mighty world, we sing to thee:
Alleluia, Alleluia!

For the evangelists, by whose blest word,
Like fourfold streams, the garden of the Lord,
Is fair and fruitful, be thy name adored.
Alleluia, Alleluia!

For martyrs, who with rapture kindled eye,
Saw the bright crown descending from the sky,
And seeing, grasped it, thee we glorify.
Alleluia, Alleluia!

O blest communion! fellowship divine!
We feebly struggle, they in glory shine;
All are one in thee, for all are thine.
Alleluia, Alleluia!

O may thy soldiers, faithful, true, and bold,
Fight as the saints who nobly fought of old,
And win, with them, the victor's crown of gold.
Alleluia, Alleluia!

And when the strife is fierce, the warfare long
Steals on the ear the distant triumph-song,
And hearts are brave again, and arms are strong.
Alleluia, Alleluia!

The golden evening brightens in the west;
Soon, soon to faithful warriors comes their rest;
Sweet is the calm of paradise the blessed.
Alleluia, Alleluia!

But lo! there breaks a yet more glorious day;
The saints triumphant rise in bright array:
The King of glory passes on his way.
Alleluia, Alleluia!

From earth's wide bounds, from ocean's farthest coast,
Through gates of pearl streams in the countless host,
Singing to Father, Son and Holy Ghost.
Alleluia, Alleluia!

original poem by
Bishop WW How (1823–1897)

Sun of my soul, thou Saviour dear

Sun of my soul, thou Saviour dear,
It is not night if thou be near:
O may no earthborn cloud arise
To hide thee from thy servant's eyes.

When the soft dews of kindly sleep
My wearied eyelids gently steep,
Be my last thought, how sweet to rest
Forever on my Saviour's breast.

Abide with me from morn till eve,
For without thee I cannot live;
Abide with me when night is nigh,
For without thee I dare not die.

If some poor wandering child of thine
Has spurned today the voice divine,
Now, Lord, the gracious work begin;
Let him no more lie down in sin.

Watch by the sick; enrich the poor
With blessings from thy boundless store;
Be every mourner's sleep tonight
Like infants' slumbers, pure and light.

Come near and bless us when we wake,
Ere through the world our way we take;
Till in the ocean of thy love
We lose ourselves in heaven above.

original poem by
John Keble (1792–1866)

What are these that glow from afar

What are these that glow from afar,
These that lean over the golden bar,
Strong as the lion, pure as the dove,
With open arms, and hearts of love?
They the blessèd ones gone before,
They the blessèd for evermore;
Out of great tribulation they went
Home to their home of heaven content.

What are these that fly as a cloud,
With flashing heads and faces bowed;
In their mouths a victorious psalm,
In their hands a robe and palm?
Welcoming angels these that shine,
Your own angel, and yours and mine;
Who have hedged us, both day and night
On the left hand and the right.

Light above light, and bliss beyond bliss,
Whom words cannot utter, lo, who is this?
As a King with many crowns he stands,
And our names are grav'n upon his hands;
As a priest, with God-uplifted eyes,
He offers for us his sacrifice;
As the Lamb of God, for sinners slain,
That we too may live, he lives again.

God the Father give us grace
To walk in the light of Jesu's face;
God the Son give us a part
In the hiding-place of Jesu's heart;
God the Spirit so hold us up
That we may drink of Jesu's cup;
God Almighty, God three in one,
God Almighty, God alone.

original poem by
Christina Rossetti (1830–1894)

Onward, Christian soldiers

Onward, Christian soldiers, marching as to war,
With the cross of Jesus going on before.
Christ the royal master leads against the foe;
Forward into battle, see, his banners go!

Chorus
Onward, Christian soldiers, marching as to war,
With the cross of Jesus going on before.

At the sign of triumph Satan's legions flee;
On then, Christian soldiers, on to victory.
Hell's foundations quiver at the shout of praise;
Brothers lift your voices, loud your anthems raise.

Chorus

Like a mighty army moves the church of God;
Brothers, we are treading where the saints have trod;
We are not divided, all one body we,
One in hope and doctrine, one in charity.

Chorus

What the saints established that I hold for true.
What the saints believèd, that I believe too.
Long as earth endureth, men the faith will hold,
Kingdoms, nations, empires, in destruction rolled.

Chorus

Crowns and thrones may perish, kingdoms rise and wane,
But the church of Jesus constant will remain;
Gates of hell can never 'gainst that church prevail;
We have Christ's own promise, and that cannot fail.

Chorus

Onward, then, ye people, join our happy throng,
Blend with ours your voices in the triumph song;
Glory, laud, and honour unto Christ the King;
This through countless ages men and angels sing.

Chorus

original poem by
Sabine Baring-Gould (1834–1924)

Now the day is over

Now the day is over,
Night is drawing nigh,
Shadows of the evening
Steal across the sky.

Now the darkness gathers,
Stars begin to peep,
Birds, and beasts and flowers
Soon will be asleep.

Jesus, give the weary
Calm and sweet repose;
With thy tenderest blessing
May our eyelids close.

Grant to little children
Visions bright of thee;
Guard the sailors tossing
On the deep blue sea.

Comfort every sufferer,
Watching late in pain;
Those who plan some evil
From their sin restrain.

Through the long night watches
May thine angels spread
Their white wings above me,
Watching round my bed.

When the morning wakens,
Then may I arise
Pure, and fresh, and sinless
In thy holy eyes.

Glory to the Father,
Glory to the Son,
And to thee, blest Spirit,
While all ages run.

original poem by
Sabine Baring-Gould (1834–1924)

Come, Holy Ghost, our souls inspire

Come, Holy Ghost, our souls inspire,
And lighten with celestial fire;
Thou the anointing Spirit art,
Who dost thy sev'nfold gifts impart.

Chorus
Praise to thy eternal merit,
Father, Son, and Holy Spirit.

Thy blessèd unction from above
Is comfort, life, and fire of love;
Enable with perpetual light
The dullness of our blinded sight.

Chorus

Anoint and cheer our soilèd face
With the abundance of thy grace:
Keep far our foes, give peace at home;
Where thou art guide no ill can come.

Chorus

Teach us to know the Father, Son,
And thee, of both, to be but one;
That through the ages all along
This this may be our endless song.

Chorus

original poem by
Bishop John Cosin (1594–1672)

Most glorious Lord of life

Most glorious Lord of life, that on this day
Didst make thy triumph over death and sin,
And having harrowed hell, didst bring away
Captivity thence captive, us to win.

This joyous day, dear Lord, with joy begin,
And grant that we may for whom thou diddest die,
Being with thy dear blood clean washed from sin,
May live forever in felicity.

And that thy love we weighing worthily,
May likewise love thee for the same again;
And for thy sake, that all like dear didst buy,
With love may one another entertain.

So let us love, dear love, like as we ought;
Love is the lesson which the Lord us taught.

original poem by
Edmund Spenser (1553–1599)

Wilt thou forgive that sin

Wilt thou forgive that sin, by man begun,
Which was my sin though it were done before?
Wilt thou forgive that sin, through which I run,
And do run still, though still I do deplore?
When thou hast done, thou hast not done,
For I have more.

Wilt thou forgive that sin which I have won
Others to sin, and made my sin their door?
Wilt thou forgive that sin which I did shun
A year or two, but wallowed in a score?
When thou hast done, thou hast not done,
For I have more.

I have a sin of fear, that when I've spun
My last thread, I shall perish on the shore,
But swear by thyself, that at my death thy Son
Shall shine, as he shines now and heretofore:
And, having done that, thou hast done:
I fear no more.

original poem by
John Donne (1578–1631)

In the hour
of my distress

In the hour of my distress,
When temptations me oppress,
And when I my sins confess,
Sweet Spirit comfort me!

When I lie within my bed,
Sick in heart, and sick in head,
And with doubts discomforted,
Sweet Spirit comfort me!

When the house doth sigh and weep,
And the world is drowned in sleep,
Yet mine eyes the watch do keep;
Sweet Spirit comfort me!

When (God knows) I'm tossed about,
Either with despair, or doubt;
Yet, before the glass be out,
Sweet Spirit comfort me!

When the judgment is revealed,
And that opened which was sealed,
When to thee I have appealed,
Sweet Spirit comfort me!

original poem by
Robert Herrick (1591–1674)

What sweeter music can we bring

What sweeter music can we bring
Than a carol, for to sing
The birth of this our heavenly King?
Awake the voice! Awake the string!

Dark and dull night, fly hence away,
And give the honour to this day,
That sees December turned to May.

Why does the chilling winter's morn
Smile, like a field beset with corn?
Or smell like a meadow newly-shorn,
Thus, on the sudden? Come and see

The cause, why things thus fragrant be:
'Tis he is born, whose quickening birth
Gives life and lustre, public mirth,
To heaven, and the under-earth.

We see him once, and know him ours,
Who, with his sunshine and his showers,
Turns all the patient ground to flowers.

The darling of the world is come,
And fit it is we find a room
To welcome him. The nobler part
Of all the house here is the heart:

Which we will give him, and bequeath
This holly and this ivy wreath,
To do him honour, who's our King,
And Lord of all this revelling.

What sweeter music can we bring,
Than a carol for to sing
The birth of this our heavenly King?

original poem by
Robert Herrick (1591–1674)

The holly and the ivy

The holly and the ivy
When they are both full grown,
Of all the trees that are in the wood,
The holly bears the crown.

Chorus
The rising of the sun,
And the running of the deer,
The playing of the merry organ,
Sweet singing in the choir,
Sweet singing in the choir.

The holly bears a blossom,
As white as lily-flower;
And Mary bore sweet Jesus Christ,
To be our sweet Saviour.

Chorus

The holly bears a berry,
As red as any blood;
And Mary bore sweet Jesus Christ,
To do poor sinners good.

Chorus

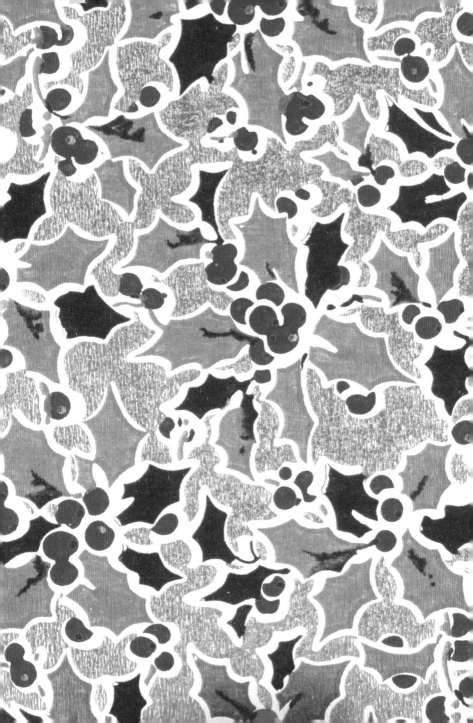

The holly bears a prickle,
As sharp as any thorn,
And Mary bore sweet Jesus Christ,
On Christmas Day in the morn.

Chorus

The holly bears a bark,
As bitter as any gall,
And Mary bore sweet Jesus Christ,
For to redeem us all.

Chorus

The holly and the ivy
When they are both full grown,
Of all the trees that are in the wood,
The holly bears the crown.

original poem by
Anonymous

A hymn of the Nativity

Come, we shepherds whose blest sight
    Hath met love's noon in nature's night;
    Come lift up our loftier song,
And wake the sun that lies too long.

To all our world of well-stol'n joy
    He slept, and dreamt of no such thing,
While we found out heaven's fairer eye,
    And kissed the cradle of our King;
Tell him he rises now too late
To show us aught worth looking at.

Tell him we now can show him more
    Than he e'er show'd to mortal sight,
Than he himself e'er saw before,
    Which to be seen needs not his light:
Tell him, Tityrus, where th' hast been,
Tell him, Thyrsis, what th' hast seen.

Gloomy night embraced the place
    Where the noble infant lay:
The babe look'd up, and show'd his face;
    In spite of darkness it was day.
It was thy day, sweet, and did rise,
Not from the east, but from thy eyes.

Winter chid the world, and sent
    The angry north to wage his wars :
The north forgot his fierce intent,
    And left perfumes instead of scars.

By those sweet eyes persuasive powers,
Where he meant frosts he scatter'd flowers.

We saw thee in thy balmy nest,
   Bright dawn of our eternal day;
We saw thine eyes break from the east,
   And trance the trembling shades away:
We saw thee (and we blest the sight)
We saw thee by thine own sweet light.

Poor world, said I, what wilt thou do
   To entertain this starry stranger?
Is this the best thou canst bestow –
   A cold and not too cleanly manger?
Contend, the powers of heaven and earth,
To fit a bed for this huge birth.

Proud world, said I, cease your contest,
   And let the mighty babe alone,
The phoenix builds the phoenix' nest,
   Love's architecture is his own.
The babe, whose birth embraves this morn,
Made his own bed ere he was born.

I saw the curl'd drops, soft and slow,
   Come hovering o'er the place's head;
Offe'ring their whitest sheets of snow,
   To furnish the fair infant's bed.
Forbear, said I, be not too bold,
Your fleece is white, but 'tis too cold.

I saw th' obsequious seraphim
    Their rosy fleece of fire bestow,
For well they now can spare their wings,
    Since heaven itself lies here below.
Well done, said I; but are you sure
Your down, so warm, will pass for pure?

No, no, your King's not yet to seek
    Where to repose his royal head;
See, see how soon his new-bloom'd cheek
    'Twixt mother's breasts is gone to bed.
Sweet choice, said we, no way but so,
Not to lie cold, yet sleep in snow!

Welcome all wonders in one sight!
    Eternity, shut in a span!
Summer in winter, day in night,
    Heaven in earth, and God in man.
Great little one, whose all-embracing birth
Lifts earth to heaven, stoops heaven to earth.

Welcome, tho' nor to gold, nor silk,
    To more than Cæsar's birthright is:
Twin sister seas of virgin's milk,
    With many a rarely-temper'd kiss,
That breathes at once both maid and mother,
Warms in the one, cools in the other.

She sings thy tears asleep, and dips
    Her kisses in thy weeping eye:
She spreads the red leaves of thy lips,
    That in their buds yet blushing lie.
She 'gainst those mother diamonds tries
The points of her young eagle's eyes.

Welcome – tho' not to those gay flies,
    Gilded i' th' beams of earthly kings,
Slippery souls in smiling eyes –
    But to poor shepherds, homespun things,
Whose wealth's their flocks, whose wit's to be
Well read in their simplicity.

Yet, when April's husband show'rs
    Shall bless the fruitful Maia's bed,
We'll bring the first-born of her flowers,
    To kiss thy feet, and crown thy head.
To thee, dread Lamb! whose love must keep
The shepherds while they feed their sheep.

To thee, meek majesty, soft King
    Of simple graces and sweet loves!
Each of us his lamb will bring,
    Each his pair of silver doves!
At last, in fire of thy fair eyes,
Ourselves become our own best sacrifice!

original poem by
Richard Crashaw (1613–1649)

A hymn for Christmas Day

Christians awake, salute the happy morn,
Whereon the Saviour of the world was born;
Rise, to adore the mystery of love,
Which hosts of angels chanted from above;

With them the joyful tidings first begun
Of God incarnate, and the Virgin's son:
Then to the watchful shepherds it was told,
Who heard the angelic herald's voice; 'Behold!

I bring good tidings of a Saviour's birth
To you, and all the nations upon earth;
This day hath God fulfilled his promised word;
This day is born a Saviour, Christ, the Lord.'

In David's city, shepherds, ye shall find
The long foretold redeemer of mankind;
Wrapped up in swaddling clothes, the babe divine
Lies in a manger; this shall be your sign.'

He spoke, and straightway the celestial choir
In hymns of joy, unknown before, conspire;
The praises of redeeming love they sung,
And heaven's whole orb with alleluias rung:

God's highest glory was their anthem still;
Peace upon earth, and mutual good-will.
To Bethlehem straight the enlightened shepherds ran,
To see the wonder God had wrought for man;

And found, with Joseph and the blessèd maid,
Her son, the Saviour, in a manger laid.
Amazed, the wondrous story they proclaim,
The first apostles of this infant fame.

While Mary keeps, and ponders in her heart,
The heavenly vision, which the swains impart;
They to their flocks, still praising God, return,
And their glad hearts within their bosoms burn.

Let us, like these good shepherds then, employ
Our grateful voices to proclaim the joy:
Like Mary, let us ponder in our mind
God's wondrous love in saving lost mankind;

Artless, and watchful, as these favoured swains,
While virgin meekness in the heart remains:
Trace we the babe, who has retrieved our loss,
From his poor manger to his bitter cross;

Treading his steps, assisted by his grace,
Till man's first heavenly state again takes place.
Then may we hope, the angelic thrones among,
To sing, redeemed, a glad triumphal song;

He that was born, upon this joyful day,
Around us all, his glory shall display;
Saved by his love, incessant we shall sing
Of angels, and of angel-men, the King.

original poem by
John Byrom (1692–1763)

Hark! The herald angels sing

Hark! The herald angels sing
Glory to the newborn King;
Peace on earth and mercy mild,
God and sinners reconciled:
Joyful all ye nations rise,
Join the triumph of the skies,
With th'angelic host proclaim,
Christ is born in Bethlehem!

Chorus
Hark! The herald angels sing
Glory to the newborn King!

Christ, by highest heav'n adored,
Christ, the everlasting Lord,
Late in time, behold him come
Offspring of a virgin's womb!
Veiled in flesh the Godhead see,
Hail th'incarnate deity!
Pleased with us in flesh to dwell,
Jesus, our Emmanuel.

Chorus

Hail the heaven-born prince of peace!
Hail the sun of righteousness!
Light and life to all he brings,
Ris'n with healing in his wings;

Mild he lays his glory by,
Born that man no more may die,
Born to raise the sons of earth,
Born to give them second birth.

Chorus

Come, desire of nations, come,
Fix in us thy humble home;
Rise, the woman's conqu'ring seed,
Bruise in us the serpent's head.
Now display thy saving power,
Ruined nature now restore;
Now in mystic union join
Thine to ours, and ours to thine.

Chorus

Adam's likeness, Lord, efface,
Stamp thine image in its place:
Second Adam from above,
Reinstate us in thy love.
Let us thee, though lost, regain,
Thee, the life, the inner man:
O, to all thyself impart,
Formed in each believing heart.

Chorus

original poem by
Charles Wesley (1707–1788)

In the bleak mid-winter

In the bleak mid-winter, frosty wind made moan,
Earth stood hard as iron, water like a stone;
Snow had fallen, snow on snow, snow on snow,
In the bleak mid-winter, long ago.

Our God, heaven cannot hold him, nor earth sustain;
Heaven and earth shall flee away when he comes to reign:
In the bleak mid-winter a stable place sufficed
The Lord God Almighty Jesus Christ.

Enough for him, whom cherubim worship night and day,
Breastful of milk, and a mangerful of hay;
Enough for him, whom angels fall down before,
The ox and ass and camel which adore.

Angels and archangels may have gathered there,
Cherubim and seraphim thronged the air –
But only his mother in her maiden bliss
Worshipped the beloved with a kiss.

What can I give him poor as I am?
If I were a shepherd I would bring a lamb,
If I were a wise man I would do my part;
Yet what I can I give him – give my heart.

original poem by
Christina Rossetti (1830–1894)

'Tis winter now; the fallen snow

'Tis winter now; the fallen snow
Has left the heav'ns all coldly clear;
Through leafless boughs the sharp winds blow,
And all the earth lies dead and drear.

And yet God's love is not withdrawn;
His life within the keen air breathes;
His beauty paints the crimson dawn,
And clothes the boughs with glittering wreaths.

And though abroad the sharp winds blow,
And skies are chill, and frosts are keen,
Home closer draws her circle now,
And warmer glows her light within.

O God! Who giv'st the winter's cold,
As well as summer's joyous rays,
Us warmly in thy love enfold,
And keep us through life's wintry days.

original poem by
Samuel Longfellow (1819–1892)

I sing the birth
was born tonight

I sing the birth was born tonight,
The author both of life and light;
The angels so did sound it,
And, like the ravished shepherds said,
Who saw the light, and were afraid,
Yet searched, and true they found it.

The Son of God, th'eternal King,
That did us all salvation bring,
And freed the soul from danger;
He whom the whole world could not take,
The word, which heaven and earth did make,
Was now laid in a manger.

The Father's wisdom willed it so,
The Son's obedience knew no 'No',
Both wills were in one stature;
And, as that wisdom had decreed,
The word was now made flesh indeed,
And took on him our nature.

What comfort by him do we win?
Who made himself the prince of sin,
To make us heirs of glory,
To see this babe, all innocence,
A martyr born in our defence,
Can man forget this story?

original poem by
Ben Jonson (1573–1637)

Appendix

The hymns and carols in this collection were originally written as poems and, in some cases, the lyrics differ considerably from the original text. The original poems, where they differ from the hymn, are reproduced below in *italic*.

The Lord is my shepherd (page 10)
(Text of Psalm 23)

The Lord is my shepherd; I shall not want.
He maketh me to lie down in green pastures:
He leadeth me beside the still waters.
He restoreth my soul:
He leadeth me in the paths of righteousness for his name's sake.
Yea, though I walk through the valley of the shadow of death,
I will fear no evil: for thou art with me;
Thy rod and thy staff they comfort me.
Thou preparest a table before me in the presence of mine enemies:
Thou anointest my head with oil; my cup runneth over.
Surely goodness and mercy shall follow me all the days of my life:
And I will dwell in the house of the Lord for ever.

Jerusalem the golden (page 15)
(Verses one and two)

Jerusalem the golden,
With milk and honey blest,
Beneath thy contemplation
Sink heart and voice oppressed.
I know not, O I know not,
What social joys are there
What radiancy of glory,
What *light* beyond compare.

They stand, those halls of *Sion,*
Conjubilant with song,
And bright with many an angel,
And all the martyr throng;

I will lift up mine eyes unto the hills (page 18)
(Text of Psalm 121)

I will lift up mine eyes unto the hills,
From whence cometh my help.
My help cometh from the Lord,
Which made heaven and earth.
He will not suffer thy foot to be moved:
He that keepeth thee will not slumber.
Behold, he that keepeth Israel
Shall neither slumber nor sleep.
The Lord is thy keeper:
The Lord is thy shade upon thy right hand.
The sun shall not smite thee by day,
Nor the moon by night.
The Lord shall preserve thee from all evil:
He shall preserve thy soul.
The Lord shall preserve thy going out and thy coming in
From this time forth, and even for evermore.

The Lord will come and not be slow (page 20)
(Final verse)

For great thou art, and wonders great
By thy strong hand are done:
Thou in thy everlasting seat
Remainest God alone.

Ye holy angels bright (page 25)
originally titled *A Psalm of Praise*
(Verses one and six)

Ye holy angels bright,
Which stand before God's throne,
And dwell in glorious light,
Praise ye the Lord each one!
You there so nigh
Fitter than we
Dark sinners be,
For things so high.

My soul bear thou thy part,
Triumph in God above!
With a well-tuned heart,
Sing thou the songs of love!
Thou art his own,
Whose precious blood
Shed for thy good
His love made known.

Lord, it belongs not to my care (page 28)
(Verse two)

If life be long, I will be glad,
That I may long obey;
If short, yet why should I be sad
To end my little day?

He who would valiant be (page 32)
originally titled *Who would true valour see*
(Verses one to three)

Who would true valour see,
Let him come hither;
One here will constant be,
Come wind, come weather.
There's no discouragement
Shall make him once relent,
His first avow'd intent
To be a pilgrim.

Who so beset him round
With dismal stories,
Do but themselves confound,
His strength the more is;
No lion can him fright,
He'll with a giant fight;
But he will have a right
To be a pilgrim.

Hobgoblin nor foul fiend
Can daunt his spirit;
He knows he at the end
Shall life inherit.
Then fancies fly away,
He'll fear not what men say;
He'll labour night and day
To be a pilgrim.

Let all the world in ev'ry corner sing (page 33)
originally titled *Antiphon*

Creator Spirit, by whose aid (page 34)
(Verse three)

Plenteous of grace, descend from high
Rich in thy sevenfold energy;
Make us eternal truths receive,
And practise all that we believe;
Give us thyself, that we may see
The Father and the Son by thee.

Awake, my soul, and with the sun (page 37)
(Verses two to four)

Redeem thy mis-spent time that's past
Live this day as if 'twere thy last:
Improve thy talent with due care;
For the great Day thyself prepare.

Let all thy converse be sincere,
Thy conscience as the noon-day clear;
Think how all-seeing God thy ways
And all thy secret thoughts surveys.

By influence of the light Divine
Let thy own light *in good work*s shine;
Reflect all heaven's propitious ways
In ardent love and cheerful praise.

Glory to thee, my God, this night (page 42)
(Verse six)

You, my blest guardian, whilst I sleep
Close to my bed your vigils keep;
Divine love into me instil,
Stop all the avenues of ill.

Through all the changing scenes of life (page 44)
(Additional final verse)

To Father, Son, and Holy Ghost,
The God whom we adore,
Be glory, as it was, is now,
And shall be evermore.

The spacious firmament on high (page 48)
originally titled *The confirmation of faith*

O thou from whom all goodness flows (page 80)
(Verses two to six)

When on my poor distressed heart
My sins lie heavily,
Thy pardon grant, new peace impart:
Dear Lord, remember me.

When trials sore obstruct my way,
And ills I cannot flee,
O let my strength be as my day:
Dear Lord, remember me.

If, for thy sake, upon my name
Shame and reproaches be,
All hail reproach and welcome shame:
Dear Lord, remember me.

If worn with pain, disease, or grief
This feeble *spirit be;*
Grant patience, rest, and kind relief:
Dear Lord, remember me.

And O, when in the hour of death
I wait thy just decree,
Be this the prayer of my last breath:
Dear Lord, remember me.

Rock of Ages (page 84)
(Verses one and four)

Rock of Ages, cleft for me,
Let me hide myself in Thee!
Let the water and the blood
From Thy *riven* side which flow'd,
Be of sin the double cure,
Cleanse me from its guilt and power.

While I draw this fleeting breath,
When my eyestrings break in death,
When I soar through tracts unknown,
See Thee on Thy Judgement-throne;
Rock of Ages, cleft for me,
Let me hide myself in Thee!

A cradle song (page 86)
originally titled *Sweet dreams, form a shade*

The labourer's noon-day hymn (page 94)
originally titled *Blest are the moments, doubly blest*

Christian, dost thou see them (page 100)
(Verses one and two)

Christian, dost thou see them on the holy ground,
How the troops of Midian prowl and prowl around?
Christian, up and smite them, counting gain but loss;
Smite them by the merit of the holy Cross.

Christian, dost thou feel them, how they work within,
Striving, tempting, luring, goading into sin?
Christian, never tremble; never be down-cast;
Smite them by the virtue of the Lenten fast;

Lord, I would own thy tender care (page 110)
(Verse five)

Such goodness, Lord, and constant care,
A child can ne'er repay;
But may it be my daily prayer
To love thee and obey.

God of our fathers, known of old (page 130)
originally titled *Recessional*

In the hour of my distress (page 154)
originally titled *His letanie to the Holy Spirit*

What sweeter music can we bring (page 155)
(verses two to seven)

We see him once, and know him ours,
Who with his sunshine and his showers
Turns all the patient ground to flowers.

Dark and dull night, fly hence away,
And give the honour to this day,
That sees December turned to May,
If we may ask the reason, say:

The darling of the world is come,
And fit it is we find a room
To welcome him. The nobler part
Of all the house here is the heart:

Which we will give him, and bequeath
This holly and this ivy wreath,
To do him honour who's our King,
And Lord of all this revelling.

Picture Credits

Page 11: The National Archives / Mary Evans Picture Library

Page 13, 40, 81, 87, 93, 94–95, 106, 117, 141, 144–145, 170, 173 and 176–177: Mary Evans Picture Library

Page 31: Weimar Archive / Mary Evans Picture Library

Page 35, 59, 77 and 111: Interfoto / Bildarchiv Hansmann / Mary Evans Picture Library

Page 103: Robert Gillmor / Mary Evans Picture Library

Page 109 and 125: Onslow Auctions Ltd / Mary Evans Picture Library

Page 156 and 167 © Medici / Mary Evans

Page 63, 159 and 163: Retrograph Collection / Mary Evans Picture Library

Pages 19, 22–23, 38, 56, 74–75, 85, 119, 128 and 139: NRM / Science & Society Picture Library

Page 148: Science Museum / Science & Society Picture Library

Pages 47, 50, 71, 135 and 175 © TfL from the London Transport Museum collection

Page 26: The Art Archive / Private Collection / Marc Charmet